Pebble®
Plus

Physical Science

Magnetism

by Abbie Dunne

raintree
a Capstone company — publishers for children

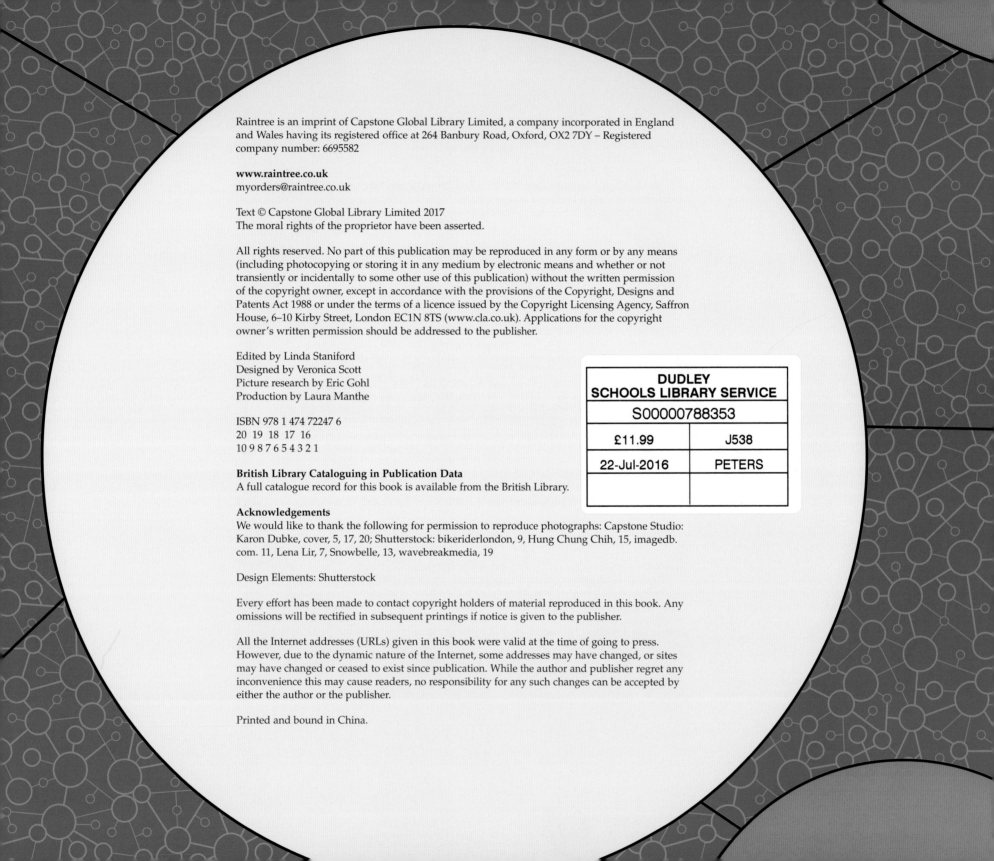

Raintree is an imprint of Capstone Global Library Limited, a company incorporated in England and Wales having its registered office at 264 Banbury Road, Oxford, OX2 7DY – Registered company number: 6695582

www.raintree.co.uk
myorders@raintree.co.uk

Edited by Linda Staniford
Designed by Veronica Scott
Picture research by Eric Gohl
Production by Laura Manthe

ISBN 978 1 474 72247 6
20 19 18 17 16
10 9 8 7 6 5 4 3 2 1

British Library Cataloguing in Publication Data
A full catalogue record for this book is available from the British Library.

Acknowledgements
We would like to thank the following for permission to reproduce photographs: Capstone Studio: Karon Dubke, cover, 5, 17, 20; Shutterstock: bikeriderlondon, 9, Hung Chung Chih, 15, imagedb. com. 11, Lena Lir, 7, Snowbelle, 13, wavebreakmedia, 19

Design Elements: Shutterstock

Every effort has been made to contact copyright holders of material reproduced in this book. Any omissions will be rectified in subsequent printings if notice is given to the publisher.

All the Internet addresses (URLs) given in this book were valid at the time of going to press. However, due to the dynamic nature of the Internet, some addresses may have changed, or sites may have changed or ceased to exist since publication. While the author and publisher regret any inconvenience this may cause readers, no responsibility for any such changes can be accepted by either the author or the publisher.

Printed and bound in China.

Contents

What is a magnet?

Magnets pull together
and push apart with a
force called magnetism.
Magnets are made
from metals.

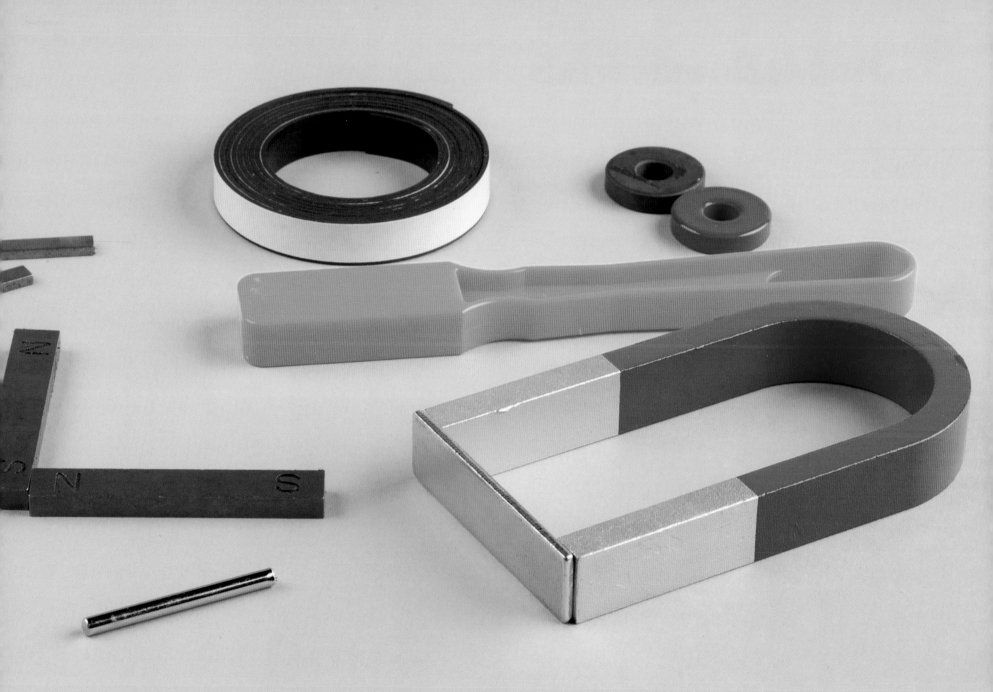

Magnetic materials

All magnets attract objects
made of iron. Nails and
paper clips stick to magnets.
Other metals do not stick
to magnets.

Magnetic field

Like a bubble, a magnetic
field surrounds a magnet.
If the magnet is close to
a magnetic object, its magnetic
field pulls the object toward it.

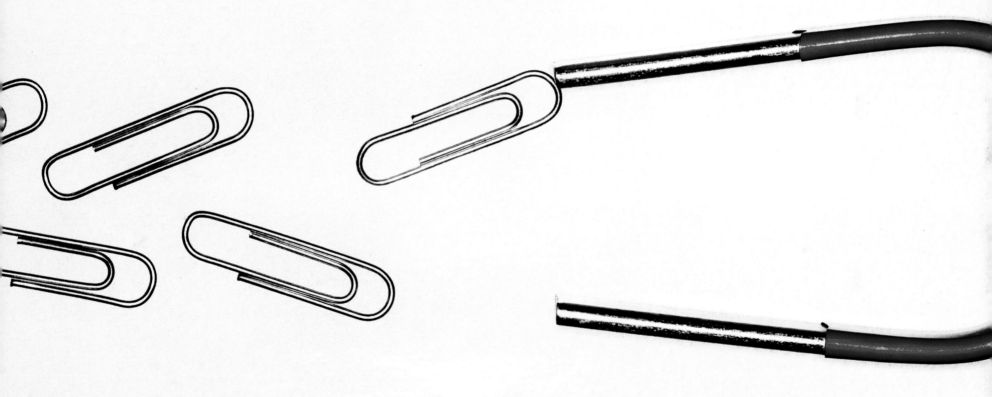

A magnet's ends are called poles. Every magnet has a north and south pole. Opposite poles attract each other. Poles that are the same repel each other.

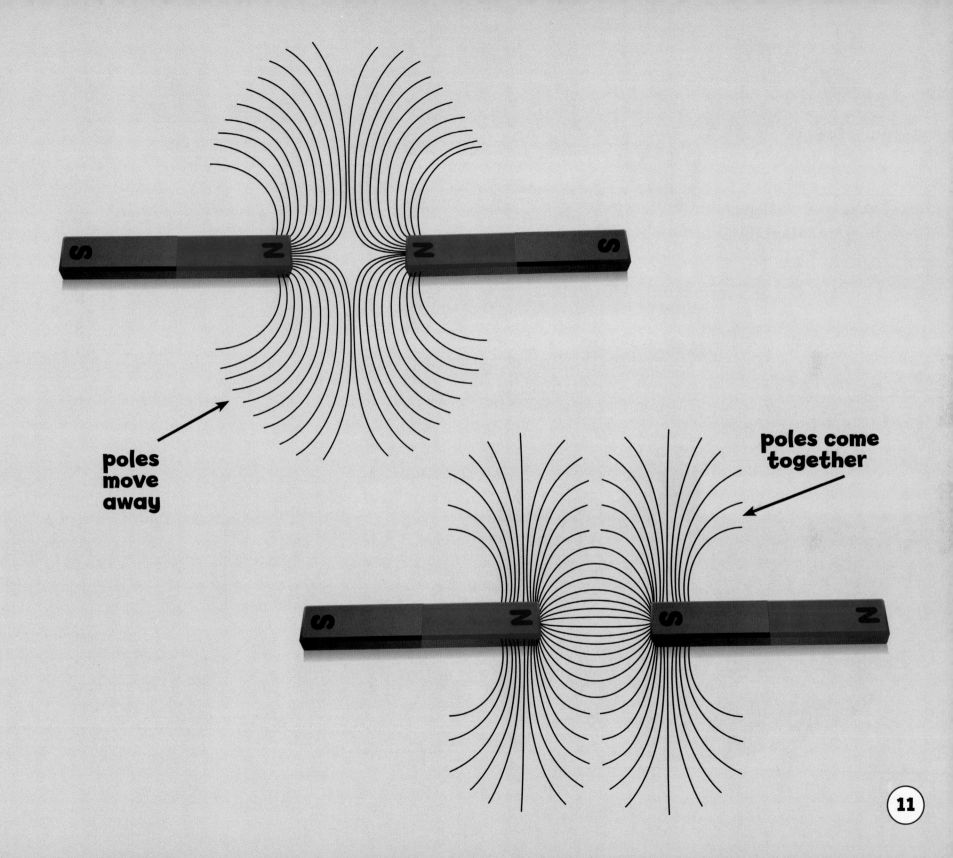

poles
move
away

poles come
together

11

Earth has an iron core.
Just like a magnet, Earth
has a magnetic field.
Earth also has a North Pole
and a South Pole.

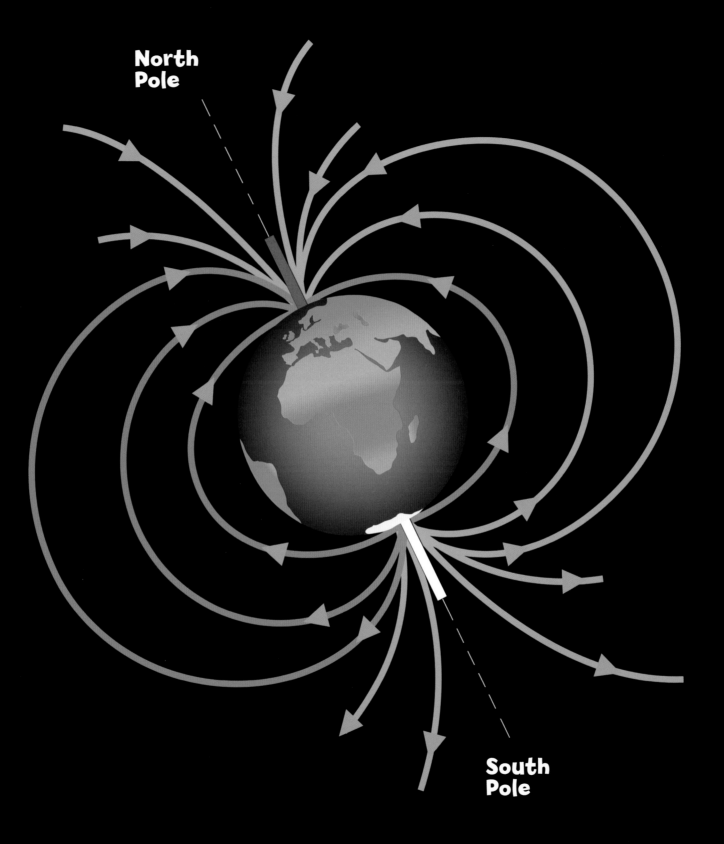

North
Pole

magnetic
field

South
Pole

13

How we use magnets

Magnets are all around us. Speakers use magnets to make sound. Magnets keep fridge doors closed. Some trains use magnets to float over a track.

A magnetic field can pass through materials such as paper, water and glass. A magnet can hold a piece of paper on to a metal fridge door.

A compass has a magnet
in the shape of a needle.
The needle moves in a circle
until it points to north.
This helps people find their way.

Activity

How far apart can two magnets be and still attract or repel each other? Write down how far apart you think they can be. Then find out!

What you need

- 2 bar magnets with north and south poles marked
- 7.6-cm x 12.7-cm (3-inch x 5-inch) index cards
- ruler

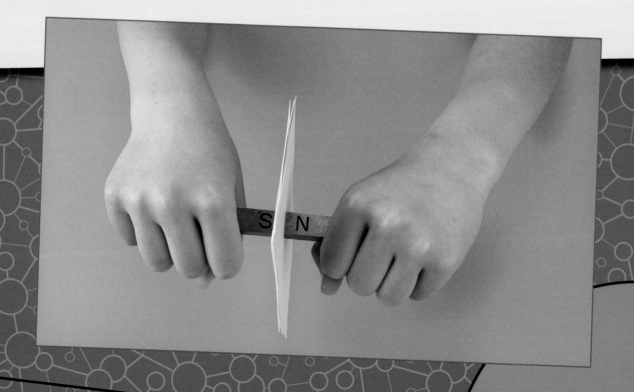

What you do

1. Place the magnets so they pull on each other and touch.

2. Put five index cards between the magnets. Wiggle the cards to show that the magnets are pulling on each other.

3. Put five more index cards between the magnets. Wiggle the cards to show that the magnets are pulling on each other.

4. Keep adding index cards, five at a time, until the magnets stop pulling on each other. Count how many cards there are between the magnets.

5. Use the ruler to measure how far apart the magnets are when they stop pulling each other.

What do you think?

Make a claim about magnets. A claim is something you believe to be true. Do magnets need to touch each other to push and pull each other?

Use facts from your test.

Glossary

attract   pull something toward something else

compass   instrument used for finding directions

force   push or pull

magnetic field   space around a magnetic object in which magnetic forces can be detected

pole   one of the two ends of a magnet; a pole can also be the top or bottom part of a planet

repel   push something away

Find out more
Books

All About Magnetism (All About Science), Angela Royston (Raintree, 2016)

Electricity and Magnets (Mind Webs), Anna Claybourne (Wayland, 2016)

Magnets and Springs (How Does Science Work?), Carol Ballard (Wayland, 2014)

Websites

www.bbc.co.uk/bitesize/ks2/science/physical_processes/magnets/read/1/

This site has lots of information about magnets.

www.bbc.co.uk/education/clips/zsg3cdm

This video shows super-powerful magnets and how they are used.

www.first4magnets.com/magnets-in-the-house-i75

This site shows where magnets are used in our homes and has lots of other fun facts about magnets.

Comprehension questions

1. If you hold the north poles of two magnets near each other, will they pull together (attract) or push apart (repel)?

2. Magnets are everywhere. Can you think of a magnet you use often?

3. Could you use a magnet to pick up an aluminium can? Why or why not?

Index